City of Song

Poems by Glenn North

Spartan Press
Kansas City Missouri

Spartan Press
Kansas City, Missouri
spartanpresskc.com

Spartan
Press

Second Edition
ISBN: 978-1-950380-17-6
LCCN: 2019937289

Design, edits and layout: Jeanette Powers, Jason Ryberg
Cover and interior photos: Diallo Javonne French

I want to thank God, the greatest poet of all, for blessing me with the gift and the desire to write; my grandmother, Louia North, for stirring that gift up; and my mother, Susanne North, for helping to sustain it. To my sister, Kellie, for her unwavering support; and to my father, Glenn Sr. for sticking around when a lot of fathers didn't. Much love to my *partners in rhyme* Marcus Brown and Jay Hawkins: *Verbal Attack is spectacular …* and to the Black Poets Collective for helping us build. Undying gratitude to Marcia Pomeroy and Michael Toombs for believing in me and teaching me to believe in myself. Gotta shout out the big homie, Dr. Charles Kovich, for helping me to get on track academically and the UMKC Creative Writing Department for helping me realize how much work I still need to do. Big ups to the my old family at the American Jazz Museum and the Negro League Baseball Museum and to my new family at the Black Archives of Mid-America, The Kansas City Public Library and the Mutual Musicians Foundation. So much gratitude to the Cave Canem family for understanding that #BlackPoetryMatters because #BlackLivesMatter and to all the fam at Brave New Voices and Louder Than A Bomb for helping to transform the lives of our youth through the written and spoken word so they can transform their communities. I ain't forgot you JKG, real ninjas know. Of course, to the visionary team at Prospero's for their investment in local talent, and to all the poets, visual artists (yes, you Sonie Ruffin), dancers, and musicians who live in Kansas City or came to visit me here — thank you for helping me in my continual desire to become a better poet and a better person.

-GN

Table of Contents

City of Song

For we are his workmanship [Greek word poiema = poem in English], created in Christ Jesus unto good works, which God hath before ordained that we should walk in them.

—Ephesians 2:10

from Ghosts Over Water: A KC Renga

This city of song:
Bird gave birth to bebop here.
Now bullets blast loud

composing dark symphonies
played for lifeless brown bodies.

Kansas City knows
terror is a tricky tune.
Like America

we still long to dance, we just
need to remember the moves.

The Lynch Family Blues

After "Lynch Family" by Joseph Hirsch, 1946

Went out swingin last night, Baby
hope you didn't wait up for me.
Said I was swingin all night, Baby
did you stay up late for me?
I wasn't swingin in no joint, Darlin
I was out on the limb of a tree.

Now I'm walkin on air, Baby
feels almost like I'm free.
My feet steady kickin the wind
yeah, I'm close to bein free.
For the first time in my life, Baby
white folks is lookin up to me.

Listen, son, your daddy loves you
keep hangin on to hope.
You the man of the house now
gotta help ya mama cope.
Daddy won't be home no more
cause I reached the end of my rope.

Defining Jazz

Jazz is …

The sound Adam made
the moment he woke up &
laid his eyes on Eve.

Jazz is …

The collective breath
of a band of runaway
slaves headed up north.

Jazz is …

The whispered relief
of southern trees no longer
leafing brown bodies.

The Prodigal Poem

This poem is unwanted.
This poem is illegitimate.
This poem was an accident.
I didn't mean to write it!
Yes, I let my pen touch the pad
but I was just scribbling
just doodling
just playing around with it
like so many other poets before me.
See, I thought the paper
was on the pill
so I didn't use any protection
no correction tape
no white out
no eraser.

I wanted to have it aborted
but by the time
I had saved up enough loot
it had already reached its 3rd stanza.

The paper won't consent
to an ink test so I'm not claiming it.
However, I see it hanging out
in the hood sometimes.

This poem lets its words sag
so you can see its behind.
This poem wasn't raised right
it can barely even rhyme.
This poem hangs out with weed papers
and it drinks too much wine.
This poem will be dead
before it reaches its 21st line —
crumpled up in some waste basket
next to a suicide letter
or tragically executed by
a heartless paper shredder.

At the very least
it will end up locked behind the bars
of some legal pad
it will be too late then
to blame it on Dad
(whoever that may be).

No, this poem won't end happily.
It has already lost touch with reality.
Heavily influenced by MTV
it's caught up in some warped hip hop fantasy
it denies the genre in which it belongs
this poem thinks that it's a rap song:

P to the izz O
E to the izz M
that's the anthem
get all your hands up!

This poem will never be published
revised or anthologized.
This poem will never reside
on a library shelf
because this poem is illiterate
it can't even read itself.

This poem could never be a love poem.
It's too busy trying to be a
mack daddy poem

but countless careless encounters
have made it a
that-just-my-baby-daddy poem
and it has left fatherless verses
in journals and notebooks all over town
with each passing line
it sinks further down.

Job, Psalm, Proverbs
and not just these
but Ecclesiastes
and Song of Solomon
yearned for this poem
to follow them.

These prophetic poems
that foretold of the coming Messiah
and the glory of the New Jerusalem
reached out to this poem
prayed for this poem
loved this poem.

But some poems
don’t want to be saved
they just crash and burn
at the bottom of the page.

I Be Black

I be black like burnt chitlins
like the pupils in the eyes of African children
the hope in their hearts
the scars on their knees
I be black like them cats on the corner
saying, *Nigga please!*
or *I wish a nigga would!*
I be black like Katrina-flooded hoods
in New Orleans.

Black like all this melanin
in the skin I'm in
that blocks carcinogens
in Ultra-Violet rays
so I can drink in the sun
on 90 degree Kansas City days.

I be black like pre-Emancipation Proclamation
southern nights when our ancestors took flight
I be black like Nat Turner's knuckles
like Harriet Tubman's feet.

I be black like the deep
of the Atlantic Ocean
the secrets it stores
like the bones of 50 million ancestors
that sunk to its floor
I be black like the scars
left from lashes
on my great-great grandfather's back
black like notes being blown
from Charlie Parker's sax.

I be black like the brown sacks
that cover cold cans of Colt 45
black like chicken wings & drumsticks & thighs
cause I love dark meat
black like the 200 brothas this year
gunned down in the streets
I be black like the pages
of the Bible that holds the key
to their resurrection
I be black like Simon of Cyrene
that bore the cross with Christ
the King of Kings

I be black like the ink I sling
like the words I bring:
an erudite manifestation of scholarly
lucidity that illuminates with the energy
produced by fiercely fervent friction.
Yes the world is scared of
my Big Black Diction!

I be black like the color
of my true love's hair
her kiss that calls me home
each night, her love that
makes me wanna do right.
I be black
like Mississippi catfish breaded
and deep fried
I'm so black
I'm black on both sides.

I see black
I need black
from Frederick Douglass to Toni Morrison

I read black
so yes indeed black
so Amistad: *Give us free* black
that when I'm cut
I bleed black.

W.B.L.K.

Thanks for tuning in …
You are now down with the sounds
of W.B.L.K., 00.0 on your FM dial
and I'm DJ Tongue Tied
here to get you through
your *Live drive at 5.*
Be sure to stay tuned
as we get you crunked up
with the new shiznit
from the crew that brought you
the number one hit
I Need A Gang-Bangin chick
It's the Blood Money Bros
with their new phat track
I Be Smackin My Hoes.

But first we have an important
announcement from the
AD HOC Group Against Crime:

Tyrone Jackson, who is Sharice Brown's
baby daddy, is missing.
Although he was spotted on the corner of Linwood & Troost
no one currently knows his whereabouts.
Sharice says: *Tyrone, if you're listening*
please stop trippin and call home.
Little baby Tyrice is running low on
Similac and he's wearing his last Pamper.

More hot jams coming up
but before we get into this next set
I just wanted to remind our listeners
we still have those free tickets to
Leroy's Liquor Lounge
and Dinner Playhouse
where this will be the opening weekend
of the feel-good musical
The Jeffersons Have Some Good Times
when They Are Reunited with Their
Homeboys from Outer Space.
Starring Sherman Hemsley, Isabelle Sanford
and Jimmy "JJ" Walker with a

special guest appearance by John Amos
recreating his role as James Evans
(who will miraculously return from
the grave in search of another job).

Just be caller #13
and the tickets are yours.
By the way, Leroy wants all you listeners out there
to make sure you try his new desert
chicken-fried watermelon.
How good is it?
Like Jack told Helen
it ain't no tellin
you gotta taste it yourself.

Now, in response to the brother
who called in earlier asking
why we never play the real hip hop
let me just say
you can't keep it real
and keep getting paid
we gotta do

what Mr. Charlie says
so you won't be hearing no Public Enemy
or no Dead Prez
no Eric B and Rakim
cause we bow down to the man
and he don't want ya'll to be thinkin
of no master plan.

See we have to mix the cuts
that keep your thoughts mixed up.
Most of our listeners dig it
even the white ones too
what KRS1 said is so very true:
What goes around comes around I figure
now we got white kids
calling themselves niggers …
just look at our call letters W.B.L.K.
We Basically Lack Knowledge
and we like it that way.

Hey! Don't you dare turn that dial
from the station that pays

we've got plenty of prizes
and more giveaways
if I announce your name
from off our fax line
you got 666 seconds
to drop us a dime.

Your prize package will include
a free lifetime subscription to Netflix
which will give you the chance
to watch plenty of great movies
like The Legend of Bagger Vance
or if Stephen King
is more like your style
call up your friends
and check out The Green Mile.

Both films are centered around
mystical darkies who use their
magical powers to benefit the
white men they love
without ever using those same powers
to help themselves.

These motion pictures will
astound and amaze
who says there are no good roles
for black actors these days.

Before we get back
to our stacks of phat tracks
this evening's weather report
is being brought to you by
Pete's Pawn Shop which carries
the diamonds you need
if you want to rock the ice
and the guns you need
if you can't pay the price.
Tonight's forecast calls for complete darkness
which should be perfectly suitable
for a community that lacks vision
and you can expect
widely scattered ignorance
in the morning

Oh, yes
and this is just in from Geechie Dave
in our traffic-copter *The Eye in the Sky*
Lack of Direction
has collided with Mass Confusion
causing a huge pile up at the intersection
of 39th and Prospect.
Traffic is backed up so far on 71 Highway
that no progress is expected
for another 400 years.

Well, that's it for your weather and traffic
now it's time to jam.
And remember
we'll keep playing the hits
as long as you keep listening …

Revival

There is a place where parched lips
kiss warped reeds and cramped fingers
stroke strings and keys
filling the air with melodies.
And resurrected rhapsodies
capture the cadence of ancient chants
where shackles are removed
and our ancestors dance
in anticipation of liberty
and every note that's played
is dedicated to their memory.

There is a place where each heartache
and every sharp pain
can be smoothed and soothed
by a medicinal refrain
the story of King David makes it plain:

And it came to pass,
when the evil spirit from God

was upon Saul that David took a harp
and played with his hand:
so Saul was refreshed, and was well
and the evil spirit departed from him.

You see this divinely inspired requiem
came forth from a glorious past
and though it defies description
we choose to call it Jazz
and ever since this music
emerged from space and time
it has found a permanent residence
on 9 + 9 and Vine.
Someday soon you'll travel there
to escape from emails
cell phones and faxes
from being overworked and underpaid
and paying too many taxes.
This is the place where even Struggle
kicks off his shoes and relaxes
and the only war that will ever take place
is the Battle of the Saxes.

This is the place where Jazz
is served up as a sensual delight
and it smells like grandmother's chitlins
cause she always cooks em just right
and it tastes like the peach cobbler
she makes that gets better with every bite
and it feels like love's very first kiss
shared in the soft moonlight
and it looks like Susanna Jones
when she wears that red dress
Lord, what a beautiful sight
and it sounds like the Jazz Disciples
smooth on a blue Monday night
or like Gabriel's trump at the Rapture
just before we take flight.

So these ministers of music
are awaiting your arrival
wanting to provide you
with orchestral comfort
as you witness the Revival
because jazz, like matter

can't be destroyed
it only changes forms
and the historic intersection
of 18th and Vine
is where jazz will be reborn.

Then we will cherish
this noble noise
and glow in the cool of its heat
as the caramel coated cacophony
creates a sonically hypnotic beat
that can only ever be heard
through the tapping soles of the feet
and as willing slaves to the rhythm
our freedom will be complete.

Borrowed Brilliance

for Charlie Parker

I was once ruled by my appetites too, man.
Got so high one night
I cried because I didn't think
anyone deserved to feel
that good. I know that constant
need for stimulation
what it's like to have your body ache
for the very thing that will cause
its destruction. But, I caught a break
found a way to kill the craving
to crucify the flesh
discovered a peace
you will never know.
And now, as I listen to KoKo
I hear you race through chords
like a schizophrenic running
when no one is chasing him.
I want to meet you somewhere in the music
to borrow some of your brilliance
for these poems I long to write.
I hope, like a junkie whose friend has just scored
that you will be willing to share.

Praise Song for Julia Lee

She was a big fat black colored girl who was just great,
and could play any request you wanted to hear.
—John Tumina, Promoter and Booking Agent

We see you, Julia, go on
wit yo fat black ass.
You are a sticky wet
street song. You are
the sweet ooze from
the sweet spot that starts
the party. You are
the Kansas City Kitty.
You pitted your big
fat, black, colored sexy
against the blonde blue.
We see you, Julia
straddling Milton's
stage, commanding the
King Size Papas to
Snatch It and Grab It.

And how they came.
How they came so
willingly to see
the epitome of a crazy little
Kansas City woman.
The song you sang made
men obey. It made
Harry Truman bring you
to Washington. Your fat
black, colored voice filling
White House halls. You lovely
lovely thing. You're still
teaching us how to swing.
You are our sexy. You are
our sultry. You are our big
fat black, colored song.

For John Coltrane

Contrapuntal #1*

with strange locomotion

    Trane transcends (sound) tracks

headed for a freedom few will ever know

    a sonic ascent beyond dissonance

he cascades a hundred notes per minute

    wielding his ax with the skill of a killer

through the thick anti-black forest

    all praises, all praises, for St. John

**A contrapuntal poem can be read top to bottom, bottom to top, with only the lines that are justified left, with only the lines that are indented, or with all four variations in a circular fashion.*

Monk

Theloniuseducescapestimesmorizestfully
dischordinarymeasuresonatetonicshifts
globalancertainspirationallurespected
adoredeemedicinalmelodiesteemancipate
harmonyxstrokestrikeystraightnochaser.

1st Minute, 1st Round: A Sonnet

(Muhammad Ali vs. Sonny Liston, May 25th 1965)

If you were a butterfly, brash and brown,
then Liston was a wing-weary moth, tricked
by the flame in your glove. 1st minute, 1st round,
like limp sex it was over just that quick.
Your phantom punch an unsuspected ping!
like Monk's finger on a startled key,
a percussive approach used in the ring
filling Liston's head with fierce cacophony.
That night there was a changing of the guard
in less than two minutes the switch occurred
the ancient Negro hit the canvas hard;
from his ashes, the new Black man emerged.
You are now trapped in tremors but I still see,
you lording over Liston like a king.

A Katrina Poem

After Faces of Katrina by Harold Smith

When thou passest through the waters,
I will be with thee; and through the rivers,
they shall not overflow thee ...

—Isaiah 43:2

The impotent levees
the crimson rain
the brown water
the hunger pangs
the August moon
the uprooted trees
the barking dogs
the siren screams
the lifeless babies
the tested faith
the delayed response
the human waste
the bright blue gloom
the broken faces
the bloated bodies

the lesser races
the blood-stained tears
the floating homes
the gnashing of teeth
the wet bones
the doomed exodus
the ironic thirst
the dripping rapes
the bullet's burst
the answered prayers
the sacred ground
the jubilant jazz
that
couldn't
be
drowned.

Sessions: The Urku* Cycle

for Sonie Ruffin and Sonia Sanchez

1.
Blood on the Water

Middle passage math =
50mil (x) 10pints per human:
can you imagine the blood?

2.
The Great Migration

Leaving everything behind
for everything ahead: Chase the moon!
The North Wind speaks of freedom.

3.
View from 12th Street Tenement

Before TV was window
watchin Lil Jazz grow up KC style—
booze, dice, hookers: his playmates.

4.
In The Blue Room

Jazz is an old lover's lips
on yours; sounds like a wet tongue plunging
deep into your hungry ear.

5.
(Synesthesia)
When Listening to Jazz

You can almost taste the blue
of a night sky, touch the star's twinkle
clearly hear the moon crying.

6.
(Dystopia)
Urban Skyline

A line of coffins across
the horizon. Bullet-riddled black
bodies. Will it ever stop?

7.
Jacob's Ladder

I too have dreams of ladders:
beautiful black bodies ascending
project steps turned crystal stair.

**An urku or "urban haiku" is an invented form which is a variation of the traditional Japanese form, haiku, with two extra syllables added to each line. The expansion of the form provides the "space" necessary to more fully express the complexity of the black experience in America. In addition, the 7-9-7 syllable count in the three lines has spiritual significance in that, according to scripture, seven is symbolic of spiritual perfection and nine is symbolic of divine completeness.*

The Art of Choking

I chew and swallow so fast
I believe choking will be
my cause of death. Just last year,
a Dorito forced its way down
the wrong pipe, its three sharp
corners, with surgical precision,
filling my throat with nacho cheese
and blood. I will never forget
the night at Gate's BBQ a jumbo-sized
rib tip was so stubbornly wedged
in my throat I couldn't catch
my breath for three whole minutes.
I lunged and bucked, eyes wide
as saucers, searching for help.
No one attempted the Heimlich.
Although the glut of meat made it
through my esophagus, it remained
lodged in my chest for two days.
But nothing compares to the time
last semester, when Sterling,

this white guy I had in a poetry
workshop, this guy who said
things like *With the inherent*
disparity that exists in the
unemployment rate it's easy to
understand why black people don't tip.
This guy that I vowed to challenge
the next time he said anything
even remotely offensive, used the word
nigger twice in one sentence
during a class discussion of the poem
Incident by Countee Cullen.
Although it came in the guise
of intellectual interrogation,
his utterance tore through me
like barbed wire through the neck
of a fourteen year old boy. But my
indignant response never made it
out of my throat. It just got stuck there
like a mis-swallowed Dorito,
or a jumbo-sized rib tip.

Check Cashing Day

for Bobby Watson

Two score and ten years ago
Martin shared a dream
for justice to roll down
like a mighty stream …

a dream deeply rooted in reality
and the solemn prospect
that he had come to the nation's capital
to cash a 100 year old check
like so many folks in the hood
with bills stacked high enough
for a bungee cord jump
anxiously looking forward
to the first of the month
with 300,000 black voices
demanding their pay
August 28th, 1963 was Check Cashing Day!

And while America had sufficient currency
in her bloated account
and black folks were only requesting
a fair amount
like frogs playing basketball on a rubber court
the check still bounced.

The first of the month has passed
600 times
since Martin uttered those
exalted lines …

I HAVE A DREAM.

We hold that phrase
in such high esteem
but there was another Martin
who also dreamed
his name was Trayvon
and along with a bag of Skittles
and a bottle of tea
his dreams got buried
six feet deep.

Slavery never really ended
it just changed forms
from sharecropping
to wage restrictions
to welfare moms.
As Martin declared in reference
to so-called emancipation in 1863
150 years later
The Negro is still not free.

A brother finally made it
to the White House
but even a black president
cannot correct
the problem of over 1 million black men
in the prison industrial complex.
Or how, like so many autumn leaves
bodies of brown boys
pile up in city streets

Yes the new Jim Crow
has enormous wings
and he loves to fly off
with colored dreams.
But back in '63
Martin also penned these lines:
Justice too long delayed
is justice denied.

And don't label me
an angry black man
because believe you me
I understand
when we follow the vision
of Dr. King
white folks are full partners
in the dream.
But in our nation's attempt
to fix the problem of race —
you ain't never gone fix
what you can't face.

So listen up, Uncle Sam,
here we stand,
with this 150 year-old check
in our tired black hands.
There's nothing left to talk about
nothing left to say
but *Cough it up, America,*
it's Check Cashing Day!

this ain't nuthin new

a twitter poem

distorted history
cant conceal
the 400yr old bloodspill
they kill
our children
tell us b patient
as they plot new ways
2 get away
w/ murder

#ferguson

Black Tide Rising

#blacklivesmatter

If you listen closely
you can hear it
when the moon sits low
full and heavy on the edge
of a blood-red sky
in that twinkling of a moment
when day is swallowed by night.

You can hear it
when the hums
of the metropolis are muted
by darkness
and the flesh of your heart
thumps against its cage of bones.

It is the distant roar
of the rising tide
a 400-year-old tide.

Racing swiftly across the Atlantic
it carries the remains
of 50 million dead ancestors.
It is teeming with the metallic taste of blood.
It knows nothing of satellites
or systems of meteorology
so it can't be traced
and it can't be stopped.
The shore cannot contain it.

This tide is deep, dark
and catastrophic.
This tide is a massive mountain
of melanin rushing
to occupy whiteness.
This tide is 39 million niggas
rollin Cadillacs over
your manicured suburban lawns
tiltin 40s in your country clubs
dickin down your daughters
fillin em with black babies.
This tide is certain.

This viscous, violent, volcanic tide
courses with the power of memory.
It remembers:

Emmet Till
Medgar Evers
Fred Hampton
Bobby Hutton
Amadou Diallo
Yusef Hawkins
Eleanor Bumpers
James Bird Jr.
Sean Bell
Oscar Grant
Trayvon Martin
Michael Brown
Eric Garner
Tamir Rice
Walter Scott
Freddie Gray
Sandra Bland

This tide knows the names
of white folks too, so watch out
Charles Koch
Trent Lott
Mitt Romney
Karl Rove
Rush Limbaugh
Bill O'Reilly
George Zimmerman
Officer Darren Wilson
Officer Daniel Pantaleo
Officer Michael Slager
Officer Timoth Loehman
Officer Brian Encinia

(and ya'll thought Katrina was bad)

This tide is supernatural.
It is seething with the paranormal ooze
of 13,000 ghosts in hoodies.
This tide is ride or die

and it collides
with the impact of 41 shots to the dome.
This wave of sea, sudsing
with holy water is a reaper.
And it ain't about rage
or revenge or even reparations
it's about retribution.
This rising tide of tears
can't be diminished, diked, or damned
and like the One who is I AM
it is as omnipotent
as it is omnipresent
which is to say
it is everywhere
so beware!

Its waves are crashing soon.

What Were Their Names?

for The Black Archives of Mid-America

When pondering origins
I sometimes trouble
the loose threads dangling
from the base of my spine
where God stitched me
in my mother's womb.

I am five years shy of fifty
but the threads are as ancient
as the Garden of Eden
coded with a language as archaic
as that which was spoken
in the Land of Shinar
when there was only one tongue
only one enormous continent.

Who was there to witness
the tectonic shifts?

Who were those scattered tribes
guided by ancient stars?

I long to know their names…
Who were they?
Erecting pyramids in Giza?
Hanging gardens in Babylon?
Worshipping at the Temple of Artemis?

Who were those
noble brown monarchs
building kingdoms
on West African shores?
There is this bubbling
in my blood
a rumbling in my bones
that longs to connect
with those who came before.

Who bathed in the golden sun
before the slave ships came?
Which proud Virginian bought them
& made them take his name?

Who were those who escaped
to freedom with their hearts set aflame?
Who were the ones
that helped them
but chose to remain?
Under the majesty
of the star strewn night
there is a hunger in my veins
there is space beneath the cosmos
that I seek to claim
it is the idea of ancestry
that becomes a soft refrain
the knowledge of my ancestors
is a treasure I must gain
someday I will find them
& learn to sing their names.

Celebration

poem written for Black History Month

Black folks know how to struggle
like trapped birds
who have filled their cages with song
like muscles that have been
torn and stretched
before becoming strong
like lumps of coal that emerge as diamonds
after being burned and pressured too long.

We struggle in style.
We suffer and smile.
We grieve and we grin.
We don't break cause we bend (and)
we never give in.

Because we know God will never
give us more than we can handle
which gets us through in the clutch.

We just sometimes wish
He wouldn't trust us so much.

Yes, we play the hand
that was dealt us with ease—
who else could turn chitlins into delicacies?

Who else could take the N-word
as much as we hated to hear it
and turn it into a term of endearment?

Who else could turn slave songs
into coded incantations
that led to freedom
from master's plantation?

Who else could take the pain
that accompanies truth
give it a soundtrack
and call it the blues?

Who else could be broke
and still dress sporty;
make a smooth entrance
even when arriving tardy
and turn an eviction notice
into a rent party?
Who else, in the midst of tragedy
and emotional confusion
could turn the sadness of a funeral
into a family reunion?
Now, the Apostle Paul told the church in Rome
what my grandmother taught me
as a child at home:

For I reckon that the sufferings
of this present time are not worthy
to be compared with the glory
which shall be revealed in us...

Now I speak with all the courage
that has been instilled in us

with the strength of the sweat and the blood
that has been spilled for us
may each season of celebration rebuild in us
what our oppressors have tried to kill in us.

Because WHO ELSE
but a great and mighty nation
could take the incessant injustice
that we have endured
and turn it into a celebration?

www.ingramcontent.com/pod-product-compliance
Lightning Source LLC
Chambersburg PA
CBHW030132100526
44591CB00009B/626
* 9 7 8 1 9 5 0 3 8 0 1 7 6 *